SATURDAY, 3PM

50 ETERNAL DELIGHTS OF MODERN FOOTBALL

SATURDAY, 3PM
50 ETERNAL DELIGHTS OF MODERN FOOTBALL

DANIEL GRAY

B L O O M S B U R Y
LONDON · OXFORD · NEW YORK · NEW DELHI · SYDNEY

Bloomsbury Sport
An imprint of Bloomsbury Publishing Plc

50 Bedford Square   1385 Broadway
London   New York
WC1B 3DP   NY 10018
UK   USA

www.bloomsbury.com

BLOOMSBURY and the Diana logo are trademarks of Bloomsbury Publishing Plc

First published 2016

© Daniel Gray, 2016

Daniel Gray has asserted his right under the Copyright, Designs and
Patents Act, 1988, to be identified as Author of this work.

All rights reserved. No part of this publication may be reproduced or transmitted
in any form or by any means, electronic or mechanical, including photocopying,
recording, or any information storage or retrieval system, without prior
permission in writing from the publishers.

No responsibility for loss caused to any individual or organization acting on
or refraining from action as a result of the material in this publication can
be accepted by Bloomsbury or the author.

British Library Cataloguing-in-Publication Data
A catalogue record for this book is available from the British Library.

Library of Congress Cataloguing-in-Publication data has been applied for.

ISBN: HB: 978-1-4729-2511-4
ePub: 978-1-4729-2512-1

2 4 6 8 10 9 7 5 3 1

Typeset in Haarlemmer MT by Deanta Global Publishing Services,
Chennai, India
Printed and bound in Great Britain by CPI Group (UK) Ltd, Croydon CR0 4YY

To find out more about our authors and books visit www.bloomsbury.com.
Here you will find extracts, author interviews, details of forthcoming
events and the option to sign up for our newsletters.

To the girl who listens at the window.

CONTENTS

CONTENTS

CONTENTS

CONTENTS

PREFACE

OR, FINDING SOME THINGS TO LOVE

It would be easy to write a book listing everything that I dislike about modern football. Lunchtime kick-offs, non-black boots, those massive headphones that players wear, sickening wages and absurd ticket prices. I could go on. Goal-line technology, the number of people who sit on dug-out benches, Robbie Savage, after-goal music, 'false number 9s', and other attempts to sully the chaos and magic of the game with science and theory.

In January 2015, the FA, television and marketing colluded to smear filthy icing on this vulgar cake: they made the FA Cup Third Round last for five days. The FA Cup Third Round. Football's Christmas. The BBC incessantly referred to the 'magic of the FA

Cup'; if they said it enough, we might just believe it. As I tried to comprehend a Third Round tie being on television in the slot usually reserved for *DIY SOS*, my mind descended into a dark place: did I even like football any more? What, beyond the fact that I am locked in an abusive, one-sided relationship with my team, kept me going along to matches, and still caring?

As with so many great thinkers, the answer came to me in a north-eastern branch of Wetherspoons. At one end of the pub was a games machine with two discarded crutches leaning against it. Perhaps a miracle had occurred during a game of *Deal or No Deal*. At the other, hundreds of old hardback books lined shelves. It was supposed to give the feeling of a private library in an Edwardian professor's villa. If you ignored the couple in the corner necking Apple Sourz, it wasn't far off. There were novels, reference works and text books weighty enough to concuss the sturdiest of County Durham schoolchildren. And there was *Delight*, by J. B. Priestley. It fitted beautifully into my wife's handbag.

I have read a number of Priestley's novels, and his 'through a turnstile, into . . . a more splendid kind of life', from *The Good Companions*, is my favourite piece of football writing. Possibly any writing, come to think of it. *Delight*, though, is a non-fiction endeavour in which a self-confessed 'Grumbler' imparts all that is good in the world. Priestley was writing his way out of despondency with grim and grey post-war Britain. In short essays, we share his delight with 'Shopping in small places', 'Frightening civil servants', the 'Sound of a football' and 111 other topics.

On the train home to Scotland, my FA Cup sickness still hovering, I began a list, the result of which is this short book. My football 'delights' try hard not to wallow in nostalgia, for that can only lead to regret at what is lost. Nor do they descend into laments for lost terraces, or 'against modern football' posturings. They are about good things that *are*. In a useful side effect, these passages go some way to explaining our nature, and I hope they are helpful in demonstrating why we are as we are, and justifying season ticket renewals.

Most of all, this book is here to remind you – when faced with five days of the Third Round or Football League 'rebranding' – why we care.

1

SEEING A GROUND FROM THE TRAIN

There is nothing in the carriage which suggests football. It's perhaps a Tuesday morning or a Thursday afternoon. There will be two or three people talking into their phones about missed meetings, or giving Paul from Sales the 'heads up' on something, or booking manicures. Others idle through free newspapers, checking the television listings ahead of another night in. Some jab at their laptop keyboard or a tablet screen. But not me: I have the vague feeling that a flicker of Edgeley Park can be caught, so I am looking out of the window.

The ordinariness of a midweek carriage helps make the spotting of a football ground from a train an act of escapism. In this setting Selhurst Park or London

Road or Gayfield – it hardly matters – are giving me a flirty glance and painting bright a vanilla hour.

I am probably the only one staring from the window, me and my lecherous eye, and the ground is grateful for that. It nods back and takes me momentarily elsewhere: my nostrils can smell fried onions, my ears hear men caterwauling about lottery tickets and programmes.

The most seductive have floodlights, iron pillars like four beckoning fingers. Catch them illuminated from some lonely night train in Coach H and the heart flutters. It is also hollowed by the feeling that life, football, is happening without me.

Sometimes the railway runs so close that I can almost touch the turnstiles. I can see details that Saturday souls, now cooped up in their offices or doing the school run, are missing.

This is a private show; only I know that the nets have been removed, that a lone groundsman is shaking his head in the six-yard box, that the physiotherapist's car is in the chairman's parking space.

And then the moment is gone. The train is pulling into the station and it is Tuesday morning again. For the last few minutes, though, I have been somewhere else.

WATCHING AN AWAY END ERUPT

It has to be a large following for the full effect. Away ends in which 143 supporters sit freckled across plastic seats don't work. When their teams score, they resemble the survivors of a shipwreck waving for help. There must be at least a couple of thousand fans for this delight. Best of all if the away end is tight to the pitch and a sell-out.

It is best, too, if the supporters have travelled far. Their day out will have taken planning, and either tight budgeting or a *carpe diem* moment with credit card to hand. They will have set out early, meaning time to drink and be merry or work themselves into a state of mind where nothing in the world matters so much as a football match. All of this adds to the explosion when their team scores, the goal in itself a justification for time and money.

Who are these away fans? Lads and lasses on the minibus, probably in their twenties or younger, with first jobs and no jobs; the man in the Audi taking a day off from management consultancy, his retired schoolteacher dad in the passenger seat. All the rest, too: old schoolmates and their cousins, exiles who left to find work, teenagers finding something to define themselves by, whole families, and pensioners with five layers on. So many different people, of course united by their team, as we know, but also sharing the raised stakes of travel and away days. It all adds to what happens when the ball goes in.

If you are watching an away end erupt then it is likely that you are in the home seats. You are probably, then, supporting your own team, and your heart is stubbed by the goal. Yet still you can find something impressive about that tremor in the far corner.

For the watcher, it happens gradually. The shot deflects in or the header bangs a post and trips over the line (the goal itself has to come from open play and matter to the scoreline, and the celebratory reaction is noisier and barmier in direct proportion to its speed, surprise and significance.) There is a one-second delay, and you see that corner leap before you hear it howl. The noise it makes is wild, not scriptable. There is the vague shape of a, 'Yyyyyyyeah . . .' which collapses into a sustained throaty holler. It lasts until the ball is back on the centre-spot and the PA announcer is ruefully announcing the scorer with the opposite of fanfare. At this point it gives way to a chant; the celebration is the orchestra tuning up, the song their first happy piece.

What makes it so good to watch is the anarchy of movement. Berserk limbs convulse. It is drunken nightclub dancing but on tightly-tiered rows. Hands are not raised for musical notes, but fists are held to the sky in salute of whichever God gave us goals away from home.

If you are watching and enjoying this spectacle, then you have probably been among it, and you will know exactly what is happening. Strangers are hugging, men are leaping from one row to the next, one or two are tumbling down the steps between seating blocks, and a fair few are at the front, engulfing players and being manhandled or taken away by men in bright coats. When it is done, and play is let loose again, shin gashes are checked and spectacles looked for.

Those among this happy bedlam are remembering why they've spent £150 they can't afford. All over again, they are reminded why they bother.

GETTING THE FIXTURE LIST

The thirty days of June and the thirty-one of July. In an odd year they drag, time is gloopy. Summer is about staging posts: players are freed and loanees go home; news of the pitch being reseeded or season ticket numbers being up; early transfer rumours; pre-season friendlies announced. Then, just before new signings, the return to training and remembering how beige pre-season friendlies are, arrives Fixtures Day. To some of us, it is as significant as a hundred sainted bank holidays or anniversaries.

In dark summers, the new fixture list is a lasso cast towards golden August, snaring it closer. Our partners for that summertime dance matter to an extent they wouldn't at any other time of the season: 'Who've you got first?'

We are able to plot far beyond that day, too. The fixture list is a map, allowing us to see where we will be in five or eight months, and perhaps even what mood we will be in at a specific time of day in February. As we peruse this menu of the nine months ahead, we will pick out certain defeats and tally up points totals. It may even be possible to identify the exact April fixture at which promotion will be squandered. There will be matches to look out for – birthday and Christmas fixtures, derby ties, fancied away trips – and the panic-inducing realisation that a cousin's wedding clashes with a home game. The list is full of innocence in its blank state now, and there is anticipation in imagining it later, daubed in plot and detail.

Though probably first seen on a phone or computer screen, the fixtures only really come true when read on paper. Home games are bold, as if they matter more, away ones emaciated. Opposition names are evocative, reading them in one go twice over is rhythmic, like listening to a poem about disappeared rural railway stations. There are surprise names that can strike up warm sentimentality, a long-forgotten old flame of a team returned to your division via unlikely promotion. These fixtures are delectable when first released, and then all over again as they appear in different forms: the grid with teams on the x and y axes, and dates in tiny boxes; the official card picked up in the club shop; the statistics pages of the programme.

Everything is brand new, all is forgiven, and names on a list represent what is possible. The release of the fixtures is a reassurance that, yes, football is coming back, and life will begin again.

4

CLUB SHOPS

Not megastores or city centre shops. These are usually – but not always – attached to the grounds of smaller clubs.

There can linger a feeling that club shops were an afterthought: often they are in an unloved corner of a stadium, or even a Portakabin. It means visiting takes commitment and sometimes a detour. The supporter has to work hard for a cheap mug sporting the club crest (which people at work always mention) or a garish team-shirt-shaped cushion. The best club shops have an air of bedlam. Two or three staff fail to serve the needs of 30 or 40 souls who have filtered in after a match, more if the team has won. Victory creates a desire among people to advertise their attachment to a club, or make a winning day last longer with the purchase of a DVD to watch at home later. Some are just there to keep warm.

The staff – very often women called Janet – have a special air for some of us still mesmerised by football: after all, they are on the same payroll as the players, they must know things . . . transfer tittle-tattle, who punched who in training.

There are shirts of all sizes hanging on the walls. Home shirts create steady interest and strong sales, a club's standard issue livery. Away versions possess an exotic, outsider chic and attract intrigue and a cult following, while goalkeeper shirts are rarely coveted curios. If you're lucky, you can find a bargain bin with last season's socks and shorts for three or four quid. Away from there, the aforementioned mugs loiter alongside other household wares branded with club badges and 'Est. 18-something-or-other'. There will be an odd collection of books, usually by local authors or ex-players, and perhaps even programmes. The dream, of course, is a separate programme hut.

A lot of the customers in a club shop are children. They know, if they support the same team as their father, that his financial logic goes out of the window when something says 'Nottingham Forest Football Club' or 'Preston North End' on the side of it. A yellow t-shirt that would be £3 in Primark is well worth £11.99 if, across the chest, are emblazoned the words 'Leeds United'. Dad suddenly has an interest in bedding, too, where a duvet design announces Barnsley's 1912 FA Cup victory.

There are moving scenes to be observed in club shops. Little girls beaming as they queue with their first club shirt on a hanger in their hands. Men finding an obscure away pre-season friendly programme they have been after for years, and then celebrating in their own reservedly chuffed way. New grandads spending a fortnight's pension on bibs, babysuits and anything small enough to fit a new grandchild and inform him or her who they support.

Club shops seem to live outside the rules of capitalist economy. For whole weeks at a time they exist with only a few customers troubling their branded doormats. They dwell away from the high street and rarely advertise outside the programme. These are old curiosity shops, eccentric and otherworldly. Let us salute the club-crested pencil case!

SATURDAY, 3PM

As I write, it is three o'clock on a Saturday and I am on edge. I should be somewhere else. A desk is the wrong place to be, a computer screen the wrong thing to be looking at. Saturday at three o'clock is the mooring in a football fan's week, his or her North Star.

The radio is on, bringing me goals every few minutes, tiny chinks of glee in Norwich and Carlisle. It takes me all over the country, playing sounds from elsewhere like a Beatles record snuck into 1960s Leningrad. It numbs some of the pain.

When I'm not at a match I have the solace of picturing what's going on. I can close my eyes and enter a shadow world of programme sellers packing up their unsold stock, burger men turning down the heat and keeping things warm until 5pm, late fans jogging for the turnstiles and worrying about their wheezes, and the crowd's collective rallying cry just before the whistle. I still wish I was in a football ground, though.

For all the distortions, the Sunday lunchtime and Thursday night kick-offs, this is football time. Instinct can't be removed by meddling television companies, and that is a quiet victory. At three o'clock on Saturdays, we know who we are, where we belong, and where we should be even when we aren't. Not everyone has that. We're actually very lucky. For us there is a fixed break from the complications and obstacles of being human: family life, test results, redundancy threats, damp walls, that last week in a month with £23 to live on, news bulletins bulging with sadness and guns.

We have an escape, whether actual or imagined, being at the match or being transfixed by Jeff Stelling, scheduled once a week between August and May. Being a football fan entitles us to a temporary, recurring retreat, a short holiday from real existence. Our lives can be in chaos and nothing seem fixed. Nothing except how we feel on a Saturday at 3pm, when we are elevated into blissful and infuriating distraction. What a privilege that is.

6

SPOTTING A FELLOW SUPPORTER ELSEWHERE

It doesn't have the same effect if the team is
Manchester United or Arsenal. There is little
surprise in noticing a Liverpool shirt in Singapore,
though if the wearer is a local then that is a whole
other charm in itself – football, the jaded world's
unifier. No, it has to be Oxford United, Tranmere
Rovers or some such.

There you are, a Colchester United supporter
visiting relatives in Fort William, when you spot
a 'Don't Follow Me, Follow the U's' sticker in the
back window of a Ford Focus. There you are, a
backpacking Plymouth Argyle devotee in Thailand.
On the beach, a man sports a club-crest tattoo. You
greet this fellow Pilgrim you have never before met

as if he were your best friend, the footballing version of saying 'hiya' to a celebrity in the street. There you are, a Notts County fan on a long weekend in New York when you spot a black-and-white-striped shirt-wearer queueing in front of you to go up the Empire State Building. Sometimes you might decide to approach these long-lost family members, because talking about potential summer signings several thousand miles from home is a wonderful thing (a warning, though: make your introduction only when such visual clues are in place and do not judge on accent alone – there is real disappointment in meeting someone from your pocket of the world who has never bothered with the team, the team you feel defines that pocket).

Or you may just wish to enjoy the home comfort of it all from a distance, and take heart in the feeling that when you support a football team, you are never, ever alone.

7

I associate traffic jams with my early years of going to football. With ten minutes to go in a match, I would watch people urgently shuffling their way out of the ground. 'They're trying to beat the traffic,' my dad would say. I couldn't believe this. Still can't. At 0–0 there's always chance of a winner, at 1–2 a last-minute equaliser to make Saturday night sing. When your team loses, at least stay until the end and shake your head or boo at them as they trudge off. Expressing your view at the final whistle is your entitlement, as players and managers will remind you in post-match interviews, passive aggression dripping through their words. And who will make sure the referee is aware of his incompetence well past tea time, if not you? That said, perhaps the early leavers are right, because they are assured of being able to listen to the results in the car.

After the final whistle, if we weren't waiting for autographs, Dad and I would run to the car and sometimes catch the *Sports Report* theme music in full swing. Now, merely whistling those thrilling, playful first few bars sprays goosebumps down my spine. The day's headlines from Arsenal and Aintree would be proclaimed, the music would cut as if grave news were imminent and James Alexander Gordon would be introduced with reverence, a dignitary being announced at a royal ball. As those moveable plastic heating vents steamed the windows and we joined the contemplative thousands in their stationary cars, Gordon took me to faraway places. It was Scotland which seemed the most romantic; all those Thistles and Albions, Queen of the South and Hamilton Academicals. I longed to find out exactly where the towns of St Mirren and St Johnstone were.

Though reality has stripped that exoticism from the experience (I now live in Scotland), to listen to the results in the confined space of a car remains therapeutic. It is the shipping forecast for us football fans. Simple rhythms of team and scoreline are soothing and transfixing. The sound is kept within the vehicle's frame, as if the score reader is sharing cosy tidings of three-alls and one-nils with only those present. There is music still in the geographies of place and mind, of thinking about other lives in other towns, of other fans suffering traffic jams in Oldham and Torquay. This is a soothing marriage: happy solitude and being part of something bigger.

8

BALL HITTING BAR

There are occasions when, defying logic, hitting the crossbar is better than scoring. The chain reaction it provokes makes that so. Hit the bar early on in the game and your fellow supporters ignite. Perhaps it is that we all imagine the 'donk' of ball-on-bar, a sound we can't hear above ourselves. It teases out of us round-mouthed 'aaaaawwwww' noises. Rueful hands are placed on heads but within seconds calamity has matured into motivation: teeth are gritted, hands smashed together at pace, and indecipherable yet hopeful cries of encouragement are hollered. The team have hit the bar early, and today we will be loud and our lads will get four. Had it gone in? A dull 1–0, 'we've scored too early', or even worse.

Hitting the bar is better than other ways of not scoring. Striking a post means higher potential for netting from a rebound, making it is a less weighty form of miss. Having a shot well saved is inferior to both – it implies that human interference can stop us from scoring, when we all know that goals, misses and wins are down to luck and us chanting. Hitting the bar just *looks* better too. The ball's elevation and path possess an innate visual appeal. Perhaps this attraction resides in the way it can thrust and soar like a rocket, and in the sense that, as football should really be played on the ground, the ball is acting disobediently.

There is variety in how a ball clatters the bar. A speculative shot or lob from distance leaves time for expectation to build. A thunderous header pounds the heart. Of course, it can be crushing: a late chance missed prompting stamped feet and desolate histrionics.

When ball hits bar, it cannons in unpredictable directions like a welder's sparks. Its part in the chaos of football should be cherished.

9

PRE-MATCH ROUTINES

There is a different feeling when you wake up on a matchday. It is not just a weekend thing. Your day is sparkling with promise and purpose, which is too rare. Even if you're expecting another defeat in a foul season, you still have the consolation of a pre-match routine. Until three o'clock, you are in control. This is *your* ritual.

It has probably taken a long time to perfect, and there is perhaps an undercurrent of superstition that any statistical analysis would undermine. Early in the day, clothing might be important. I wore the same boxer shorts to all Middlesbrough home matches between 1995 and 1998, in which time we were promoted twice, relegated once and lost three Cup finals.

Then the morning must be filled with the matchday habit – a walk to the shop for a paper, a chat with the newsagent about the coming defeat you can feel in your bones (you say this only to absolutely guarantee victory); a bacon sandwich in the usual café, with ketchup falling onto the fixture list you are studying.

That morning is merely a support act. When noon ticks close, the real day begins. This means taking the usual transport at the usual time 'into town'. Or, if you're one of those people I feel disproportionately jealous of, you live within walking distance of your team's ground and can saunter there like some blessed L. S. Lowry character in modern shoes. Still, though, you'll use the customary route to the pub. In that pub, the bussed-in, the hand-delivered by train and the Lowry strollers meet. It has to be the normal boozer, even if it isn't quite the same since that new landlord took over. You probably don't drink here at times other than matchdays, and so the bar staff and your fellow denizens are fortnightly acquaintances. Not quite friends, but on nodding terms. You will be meeting the usual few – dads, aunties, best mates or football mates, your conversations swaying between poorly children and lone strikers.

Then the walk to the ground. Same time, same route, same speed. Same programme, fanzine or lotto ticket seller. Same laugh at the odd-looking fella selling pin badges, same story about the time you got food poisoning from *that* burger van. Same turnstile, same stairway, same shuffle along the seats or to your place on the terrace if you're lucky in that way, and same hellos to yet more fortnightly pals. Then kick-off comes and you lose control of things.

This may be very different to your pre-match routine. You may go straight to the ground. You may even watch your team completely sober, making you a stronger person than me. As life changes so do these customs: that gloomy pub is no good for the son you need to bring to games; a concerned medical opinion kiboshes a 2.45pm cheeseburger with onions. Whatever your order of service, there is comfort in known faces and the performing of ritual, and bliss in the thought that football is about so much more than the match.

10

THE FIRST DAY OF THE SEASON

The Friday night can feel like Christmas Eve, the Saturday morning a birthday. All is brand new, a fresh year that smells of mowed grass. The torment of summer is over, purpose is back. The Sunday newspapers are worth reading again.

Rituals are renewed and even updated. Once more we have somewhere to be. Even if we're not going to a game, we have our 3pm and 5pm anchors. We can check the team line-ups and listen to the scores, life is stable, the empty chaos of aimless weekends done with. If we are going to the game, we bounce towards the ground like some princess awoken from a coma: 'Hello, trees . . . hello, birds.' There are changes, new things, to be spotted – a lick of paint on the main stand beams, a new-look, 'revamped' matchday programme, new people to sit near, new signings to be judged. The game starts, and even the misguided innovations of football authorities – foam sprays and their ilk – seem nearly exciting.

Everything is possible, the canvas blank and ready to be danced across with colour. Last season has faded away, scheduled forgiveness complete. The first day of the season is the start of yet another nine-month fling, besotted and full-on for now, but usually petering out beneath the high expectations of Christmas.

The stadium announcer is as reassuringly irritating as before – some constants are needed. When the teams emerge everything belongs to you again. The colours seem sharper, redder reds and bluer blues. There are special welcomes for those new players who, centre-circle arms aloft, clap back. Your lads dart into their positions, a firework of flesh and intention. The opposition barely exists. Intrusive, real life, the type lived from mid-May to mid-August, has melted away. The referee puts the whistle to his lips and with a roar does this life begin again.

11

SLIDE TACKLES IN MUD

I don't like perfect football pitches. They are perhaps acceptable in the early days of a season, or for your first ever match, but they detract from the game by lessening the chance of a delightful slide tackle in mud. When the grass is angelic, it irons kinks flat, robbing the play of the unpredictable. There are no strange bounces leading to goals against the run of play, no divots to befuddle a goalkeeper, and, worst of all, no tackles in which a central midfielder goes to ground somewhere near the centre-spot and ends at the centre-circle, his opponent suspended high in the cold air.

Such challenges can work to an extent on greasy green turf too, but there is something less tangible or satisfying about that, like sunbathing on pebbles rather than sand. Football suits bad weather, and the saintly slide tackle in mud is proof of that.

This does not come from a desire to see injury. In fact, the second-best slide tackle in mud is followed by the felled player bouncing immediately to his feet and squaring up to the felon, neck veins pulsing. The best is executed perfectly. The tackler must have at least a few yards of a run-up, and all the better if he has bolted across a pitch – oh, and what joy if he is lavishly out of position, a rarely lionhearted winger, perhaps. The theatre is enhanced if – and this is usually the case – he is atoning for an error or unlucky miss. He needs to be side-on to lend the appropriate shadowy air of pickpocketry, the opponent surging forwards unaware that he is prey. When the moment of ambush comes, when the tackler slithers in, it is already too late. Ball is rustled and man tumbles. It could be a solid toe that greets the ball but, when all is right with the weather and the world, a full foot's worth of leather will thud and thwack. Geographically, the greatest of these treasures is to be found by the touchline, so the passage of play can be killed, and the tackler can jog away grinning inside, his crowd rumbling as loudly as they would for a goal. To complete the piece, his opponent must remain floored. He is knowingly, squarely beaten, and there is even an air of resigned respect in the way he sits and pulls straight his socks.

Mud is important. It means a winger can't fly as he might. It means the ball turns more like a cog than a wheel. It means the tackler's skid has enough distance and speed to create anticipation and animate a crowd. Bring on the patchy pitches of February, I say; they make slide tackles, and slide tackles show that footballers – like us – care.

12

WATCHING YOUTH GAMES IN THE PARK

All through the week, the sacred pitch is buried beneath humdrum deeds. Dogs pelt after tennis balls where the goal-frames should be, and seven-year-old girls make a game of promenading along the faint touchline, paying no attention to the studmarks beneath them. If it's Monday or Tuesday, there are probably traces of this place's real purpose – discarded bits of plastic tape by the penalty spot, stiffening orange peel or mud-grids from the bottoms of boots clacked together post-match over the pathway. These are the artefacts of weekend dreaming.

On a Sunday, however, the occupation ends and such lands as these are returned to their true owners: the weekend lads and lasses who call these neglected fields home. They care so much that they hardly notice sleet or freezing toes. Rigor mortis is worthwhile for the upkeep of an unbeaten run.

If your timing is right, then the warm-up will be underway. Sometimes this will mean cones, drills and bibs. There is pleasure to be found in watching the seriousness of a tracksuited manager ferociously conducting exercises, some 56-year-old taxi driver who secretly believes that if his team wins enough promotions, then fairytales will happen to him. At other times, it will mean the joyful anarchy of schoolboys acting like a colony of hamsters in a playpen: some welting shots at a shivering goalkeeper; some drudging apathetically through leg stretches; some having a precious last can of Red Bull; some chatting about maths homework or box sets. You may even chance upon a pitch containing only one team. A gang of them will be staring at the empty half beyond, secretly hoping that the opposition isn't going to show and indulging in a collective eye-roll when they do.

The referee – a portly sort who can't believe he is still bothering, or a young officious lad with gelled hair, or a parent pretending to be reluctant – stands by the centre-spot and summons the captains with his whistle. Because he will often be blowing it on a tender morning, it shocks the air and makes crows cringe. The skippers shuffle forward, sometimes with a proper armband from a sports shop, sometimes with a re-purposed bandage, sometimes with nothing other than a cocksure captain's gait. Tails are called and four-four-twos assembled. Hands as cold and hard as street cobbles at midnight are bashed together and accompanied by screams of 'COME ON, LADS', the haka routine of park football.

Another peep from the referee and the extravaganza begins. Double geography first thing is a lifetime away – play football and seconds stretch, time is chunkier. You are elevated away from all of the usual hormonal terrors of adolescence. Nothing matters but cries of 'Man On!' and making triangles. On the sidelines, an angry breed of dads shout, but you don't hear. You're in a battle with a niggly lad from that rough estate across town, or you're trying to keep up with a wily number eight who, rumour has it, is being scouted.

To watch these distractions and battles is to be treated to a temporary exhibition. As lads and lasses move on and outgrow their boots, it could be that you are watching their last links with their younger, freer selves, selves that innocently thought it possible to be a professional footballer. Savour, then, the sound of headers being undertaken with eyes closed, and of studded herds stampeding over hard grass. Here is rampant escapism, free to watch on a park near you.

13

CARRYING ON REGARDLESS

Midnight has been and gone and the front room is getting cold. I am drifting in and out of sleep on the sofa, intermittently watching television highlights from a round of Europa League games. My eyes close in Monaco and open again in Minsk.

Some of the teams I have never heard of and have to look up. Most have diacritical marks above letters in their names, which make them feel impossibly foreign: Skënderbeu (Albania), Qarabağ (Azerbaijan) and Plzeň (Czech Republic). It is wondrous to imagine that people in places I have never heard of feel the same as me about football, and have their own delights.

I am just about awake when the programme magic-carpets me to Thessaloniki, and PAOK versus Borussia Dortmund, black versus yellow, the moon versus the sky. PAOK's number 11 scurries beyond a full-back and smashes the ball into the net via the crossbar. The power in the noise the home crowd makes seems to shake the television camera. It is an instinctive, boisterous, hedonistic roar. Number 11 hurdles advertisement boards and runs to his crowd. Men climb a fence to show rugged gratitude, beating their chests, mouths wide open and hollering to the stars. Nothing else matters. Then I remember that, if you asked any rational person, it probably should.

It *should* matter, they would say, because this is Greece, and Greece, we are told, is collapsing. All is chaos, chaos around the number 11, who is booked for over-exuberant celebrations, and chaos around the fans in orgasmic raptures. Worklessness, empty shelves, emptier cash machines, medicine running low.

Still, the players toil and conjure with artistic freedom, fans tie scarves around their wrists and light flares. Perhaps football is a distraction. Or perhaps the economic and political crumbling of a nation simply does not matter so long as there is football in the world. We supporters have our refuge from anything wretched, vicious reality hurls at us. Inside the stadium, we are protected, and removed from real life. We are the child with her hands over her ears refusing to believe in school.

All through the years, football has carried on regardless. Wars, revolutions and tragedies, on she rumbles. Even in this country, now, you can attend a game during a national crisis and hear no one talking about it. To us, watching or playing football is a natural thing to do or turn to when all else grows perilous, like a strong leader or a hiding place. The sea could flood most countries into near oblivion, but if we can find a patch of grass and something vaguely round to kick, all will be well. What a warm blanket football is.

14

BELONGING

It brings contentedness unexpectedly. There I am, waiting for a bus when it swarms over me. I become aware that, no matter what happens in the many departments of life, I belong. If all else goes awry, I will still have a football club, and it will still have me.

This must be how the religiously convinced feel. It is a faith, matchdays a service for the congregation. Clubs are omnipotent, carried in your heart on weekdays, holidays and during the dreaded summer interval. It is something to define yourself by, like an extra part of your name or your accent.

Belonging seeps into your moods. It is obvious how this is so after a win, loss or draw. Many times have I been accused of being distant, or even deep, when actually the football part of me is hurting after an unexpected home loss. On other days, the chiding of low crowd figures in a newspaper article can see afternoons lost to anger, as if a beloved auntie has been slandered. Conversely, wrapping oneself in cosy thoughts of yesteryear goals means transformative warmth. If you belong then dull hours can be lit and tedium suspended without a ball having been kicked. I've filled screeds of free hotel notepads with best elevens and lists of every Middlesbrough right-back I've seen, animating the dreariest of conferences.

Aside from those moments of connection at funerals or in faraway pubs when you meet a fellow traveller with the same attachment as yours, all of this is lived alone. It is, perhaps, what makes going to the match with thousands of your comrades so profound. As you stream towards the ground, in every step there is unity among weekday aliens. You may be completely incompatible with them elsewhere, but here you march together bonded by colours. Players, managers, owners just drop by – this is *your* club, jointly cultivated by 30,000 hearts.

'Remember the wisdom of the ages,' says the Singer at the end of *Caucasian Chalk Circle*, 'that everything belongs, by right, to those who care for it.'

Not always do you agree on team selections or set-piece takers, but when you share roots like this, there is more to unite than divide. You sing together with strangers, unthinkable elsewhere, and clutch them clumsily after scoring. Stand and take a look around: this belonging crosses class, age, gender and racial divides. What a delight it is never to be truly alone.

15

FAT PLAYERS

This is not in a derogatory sense. It is a salute to the kind of player who has slipped from the mainstream but can be found haunting lower divisions, usually in centre-midfield. He is no more corpulent than most of the crowd barracking him. He possesses the early suggestions of a plentiful belly, primed to one day gloop over the waistline of his shorts, but he is far from obese. Make him put on a football kit and play in front of a paying crowd, though, and he mutates into a jogging bear. Everything is 'Who Ate All the Pies?' and, 'He's got bigger knockers than our lass.' But boy can he play.

The barrackers realise first when a ball thunders towards him and he stuns it dead. Then there are the passes. He sprays and spatters them about, giving wingers fuel and forwards hope. Some float for 50 yards, others spin to a full-back rolling forward unseen by anyone else. When he gallops over to take corners, his chest palpitating, they shout abuse but they judge admiringly. If he is near enough to goal during the time of an attack, then mercy to the goalkeeper whose hands are burned by the embers of his pile-driver.

Could he have played higher up the game had the paunch not always gone before him? Perhaps. Yet there is cheer in the way his normal physique – mirroring that of the supporters – kept him theirs to savour.

16

JEERING PASSES THAT GO OUT OF PLAY

So many good things about football are doused in *schadenfreude*. Rivals losing, opponents being sent off, players you particularly loathe being arrested for nightclub incidents. As distasteful to normal human beings as this is, it does add another rich crust to the supporting life. Imagine instead that we indulged in the opposite to *schadenfreude*, '*mudita*' – deriving happiness from others' wellbeing. We would applaud our city rivals when they won the league and be happy for a club suddenly caked in Middle Eastern or Russian money. What a sickly, grey world. It would deduct from the experience of following a team, dampen a healthy human fire. Think how few great love songs there would be if cuckolded men smiled and shook the hands of their conquerors.

Jeering passes that go out of play is a small but important example of this. It does not bring the euphoria of celebrating a goal, instead it breeds a tickled smugness. If it happens very early in a match that matters, it can be read as a sign that this will be your day. This is so much better if the perpetrator is a star centre-forward. With his back to goal and a centre-half sniffing, he attempts to play the ball out to his winger. It rolls straight out of play for a throw-in. The attacker blames someone else, but already the jeer is ringing. It is very often an 'aaarrrggghhh' noise which, performed in unison, throws up the soundtrack of stocks day in a medieval Somerset village. Some supporters will even stand to exhibit their glee more fully, one or two arms aloft, hand signals clear.

There are other variations. A wild shot which ends up going out for a throw pleases; a goalkeeper's scuffed kick from a pass-back too. What a happily horrible lot we are.

17

CATERING VANS

Every Saturday, and on those sainted weeknights when there is a match, a fleeting community settles outside our football grounds. They bring with them temporary street furniture, and disappear shortly after the game has ended, a circus leaving town. There are decorating tables repurposed as scarf stalls, with pin-boards propped behind them. 'Get your hats and scarves, hats and scarves here,' barks a man. He often has a non-local accent and unruly facial hair, and always a money belt. The pin-badge purveyor has one too, and awkwardly bears a hat promoting his wares. Both occasionally jog on the spot to keep warm. The lotto seller has nothing but her bright jacket and fingerless gloves, the programme boy or girl a tin rectangular block to hide behind and a margarine tub of change to rifle through. There might be the odd 'promo girl' handing out flyers for a club night or a quick loan. The road behind her is tiled with her leaflets, discarded by hoards striving to think of nothing but wins and points. Three or four volunteers unused to football crowds rattle charity buckets half-full of clinking copper and nickel. Flanking all of this like smouldering sentry tanks are the catering vans.

Rarely brand new, these wagons are called things like 'Sizzle Spot', 'All Star Grill' and 'USA Burger', those names displayed in bright typefaces rarely seen away from seaside towns. A secondary line – sometimes in different lettering again – will tell you that they serve '1/4 Pounders Jumbo Hot Dogs Cheeseburgers' at the very least, and possibly even 'Chips' or 'Bacon Rolls'. While the scarf, programme and lotto mongers provide a soundtrack, the vans award the football air its scent. Fried onions never smell this good – this *poignant* – anywhere else. Memories are entangled in the odour.

Getting close to the vans, you will hear that they make noise too. Generators whir, meat sizzles, men who should know better agree to double their burger, their faces suddenly back in the school canteen line nicking chips. Seeing these crackling wagons, whether from afar or from the queue, adds to a sense of occasion. They are not usually there. Something is happening that doesn't happen every day, and that something is football. If this is indeed a night match, then the egg-yolk glow of the van's serving hatch brings theatre.

I wonder sometimes about the people who work in the vans. Do they prefer the football to the car boot sale or the village carnival? These businesses are usually staffed by one older and one younger person, who I always presume to be family. It is a pleasantly long way from a teal truck where hipsters sell Japanese dumplings for a fiver each. May the burgers of the Snack Shack stay bulk-bought, the cheese from Licensed to Grill sweaty and orange. Biting into a slightly crispy patty that has been piled up since one o'clock says 'football' where 'hand-pulled pork' does not.

Catering vans matter because they are a part of the ritual and the temporary circus. They colour the air with evocative scents, adding another, beguiling texture to our football world.

18

GOING WITH DAD

It catches me by the throat. I am walking to a game and I see their outlines. A dad and his son, going to the match. Sometimes Grandad is there, holding the line. Son wears the shirt, Dad his weekend jeans, Grandad something sensible and dark green. Of course, there are variations on this – mums and sons, dads and daughters – which are to be cherished. But father and son is what I have lived, and so it is this which brings me such particular delight.

Like a million boys and girls before me, I probably wasn't included in the attendance figure for my first ever game. It was the late 1980s and I was lifted over the turnstile and into the ground. It feels too recent for that practice to have still been rolling on, a pixel of black and white in an HD world. It was the grotty tail-end of 'old football', with all its ambrosia and poison. I am pleased to have known it, but then I remember that first flash of lime turf rather than urine trickling down terraces and Sergio Tacchini on the rampage. My dad did the lifting and for the first time we watched a football match, me roosted upon an iron-red crash barrier. Nowadays, there are seats beneath us, but we still go together. We are too far gone to take up another pastime, embedded in this pleasant paternal rut.

Going with your dad means access to a source of calm and cynicism. We are one-nil down and I am edgy. They hit a post. 'Turning point, that,' says Dad, 'we'll be fine.' We are one-nil up and I am ecstatic. They hit a post. 'It's coming, this bloody equaliser.' Dads don't always sing along, nor go quite as berserk as you after a goal. They offer the solidity of wisdom, having seen more games and shaken their heads at more players than you. At football, dads are buoyancy aids.

Football offers fathers and sons something to do together. It is a strange way of saying 'I love you', but a way of saying it nonetheless.

19

JIMMY ARMFIELD'S VOICE

Sometimes when Jimmy Armfield isn't speaking, I swear I can hear him smile. The radio commentator will have described a fine passage of play, and I just know that Jimmy is there, sitting back, arms folded, still enraptured by the game.

His voice is a blessing not only because it helps us float happily to sepia days, but also because it conveys his continuing adoration of football. For all its distortions, when 22 men crowd around a ball it's clear not that much has shifted and football remains a happy distraction.

This wouldn't work in any old voice. While the content of Jimmy's words is in itself rich, delivery is key. His regular tone is soft but serious, a measured grandad explaining why stealing is wrong. Volume rises to express annoyance at a cynical foul or glee at a wave of attacking play from a team chasing a goal. When this happens, Jimmy's voice begins as peppered rifle fire and ends with a grenade, launched after a short pause in the form of a word like 'disgrace' or 'wonderful'.

Proclamations like those are helped by a homely Lancastrian accent which throws a cloth cap upon each word as it ascends from the radio speaker. It is reassuring, a handshake between England's old and new. Set against the jarring platitudes and rent-a-voices of other pundits, Jimmy is a nice cup of tea when all around us is Blue WKD. His is a burring brogue which resonates with depth and honesty, where so much else now is sensation and surface.

When I hear Jimmy Armfield's voice I feel like I am listening in on an impromptu love letter to the game. He may only be describing a dubious offside decision, but it comes from such a tender place that I can't help but be moved. Armfield remains bewitched and besotted after a lifetime of football: there is hope for us all.

20

HEADERS

There are towering defensive headers that make the crowd feel safe, and knock-downs from the big man up front. There are near-post flicks, unmet headers across goal, and point-blank blocks, looping headers and diving ones, rarest of the rare though they now are.

Headers won in shirty tussles, neck muscles pulsating, are Herculean duels. The headed own goal is an art form in itself, especially when accompanied by the cruel ritual charade of the victim lifting his hands to his head, turning to face the halfway line and swearing aggressively and yet forlornly. As he has shown, precision is often found hiding. Headers are another element of the wonderful mess that this game is. They can jolt in any direction, spin and twist dangerously or gloriously if misjudged, bringing gleeful whoops of 'Fifty-pence-piece 'ead!' from the occasional spectator.

But the well-timed run to meet cross or corner and thud the ball into the net receives a special kind of roar. Those players who make this a specialism, those who can 'hang in the air', occasion misty-eyed looks of reverence. Supporters become sentimental onlookers observing a craftsman at work.

Oddly, it seems to me that a header is often scored when a team is two or three goals down. The scorer stalks the ball into the net, retrieves it – if you're lucky there is a barney with an unyielding goalkeeper as he does so – and bombs back to the halfway line. Somehow, that the ball has been headed douses the goal in more hope than if it had come from a one-on-one or hooked shot. The ball is dreamed into the net.

Few manoeuvres in the game are as durable as heading the ball. It represents both the clumsier and more basic side of football and the majestic, with the same result. To hear the thwack of a park-player's forehead on a size-five ball quickens the heart; to watch a nuanced flicked header by a world star flummox the goalkeeper does the same. To rise and win the challenge, to glance a header goalwards – all of it lifts any match.

21

FLOODLIGHTS

They are merely lamps in the sky, and yet they turn football into a fairytale. Floodlights say 'once upon a time' and sprinkle upon their surroundings an otherworldly sheen. Walking towards them on some winter Tuesday night puts you under a spell, renders you as simple as a moth, calls you to prayer. They are the light at the end of a tunnel.

Floodlights transform everyday streets into something else altogether. They fling an ivory shroud of reflection across tiles and bricks, making Victorian terraces into film sets. All fulgent roads lead to the ground, that neon alien ship to which we swarm like 20,000 ETs going home. Roll up, roll up, for here is glamour, showbiz, theatre and, tonight, whoever the team and whatever its fortunes, this is the only ticket in town.

If that outer-ground pageant no longer survives everywhere, then what happens next does. You push the turnstile and soon the radiant green of the pitch tickles your eyes. In comparison to a match in daylight, senses are heightened. The crowd seems louder, the air closer, burger stands more fragrant. It can even happen in daytime, once the clocks have gone back – a Saturday 3pm game that kicks off as a bright autumn day and ends under floodlights, groggily turned on midway through the second half like last year's Christmas tree bulbs. On those days do you realise that the season has really begun, that the league table may not be lying. No season is fully alive until you have glanced upwards and watched arrows of electrified rain darting through a floodlight's glow.

It is obvious to say that the greatest floodlights are of the classical type. Four pillars marking each corner: concrete plinths, iron pylons and a rectangle of a dozen or so bulbs. When observed on a town's landscape, it is this kind of floodlight that can make you sigh happily, and this kind of floodlight which may be used instead of a map to locate a ground new to you. Yet all types have charm and pull. I have a particular fondness for lights attached to the roofs of stands, which remind me of the lamps on miners' helmets. They also fail more dramatically, almost in sequence, on the rare occasions that that now happens (standard required response: 'Someone's forgotten to put 50p in the meter.').

It seems a shame, however, to even approach being technical or specific about floodlights. Their genius is in the crackle they create, the sense of expectation they rouse. *Football under the lights.* Evocative words of magic and wonder, like 'Christmas Eve' and 'seaside town'.

22

TALKING TO AN OLD MAN ABOUT FOOTBALL

He could be a relative or a family friend, or perhaps a stranger in a pub. He finds out that you are under football's spell and launches the time machine in his head. Backwards it reels, the nineteen-eighties, seventies and sixties . . . mere leaves in the wind. It settles in a place not quite recognisable as a fixed, defined decade or period, more a black and white country of long baggy shorts and crowds of 50,000 people in hats. Look hard enough into his eyes, and you can go with him.

Those old eyes, often saddened by the ailments of ageing and the passing of friends, sparkle. His younger self fights its way to the fore, the irises a portal for a version of him presumed gone. A deep, definite smile washes his face clean of worry and creases, rosy cheeks climbing as he speaks. There are slow, wistful tilts and tics of the head, each shaking free a memory. He takes you to see his heroes, his finest afternoons and his favourite places.

You are with him up the crumbling steps and in his father's arms as he is bundled into the ground. You see the same blazing green beyond a society of bobbing heads, and jostle your way down to the front to stand on a lemonade crate. You quiver every time the crowd surges, totter onto the cinder by the pitch after a goal.

Strain hard enough, and you can see the great sides winning week after week, the record victories, the games in snow, savage tackles, heavy laced balls that hardly bounce, Christmas derby matches, gentleman players with side-partings, brown boots that safeguard ankles, goalkeepers without gloves or fear, wizard dribblers and half-backs who can kick a ball to Saturn. This memory game is made of such otherworldly legends. The old man tells you of 'characters', those purveyors of derring-do and escapade. At various times, I have been treated to an

Alloa centre-forward who rounded a goalkeeper and asked the crowd where in the net they wished to see the ball dispatched, a Barnsley midfielder who would hop over the heads of full-backs, and a Raith Rovers winger so quick he could head his own crosses.

The old man has heroes, men of class and style, pith and moment. They are alive in his head, the way they moved, ran and dropped a shoulder. Should the opportunity arise, take time to listen, to shut out all the world and fix on those twinkling eyes, and you will find a game not so remote. Football, as he will repeatedly remind you, has changed. Delightfully, the way we love it hasn't.

23

VISITING A GROUND FOR THE FIRST TIME

This can be as a visiting supporter, but is perhaps best appreciated as a neutral, when you have a rational mind and an open heart. It is an adventure, and an experience at once familiar and alien, like eating your favourite meal with another family in their home.

The greatest experience involves a town centre ground with floodlights. A modern chain stadium is satisfying, and many are growing pleasing warts and developing rusty new personalities as they age, but to peer between terraced streets and catch glimpses of Goodison Park or Bramall Lane's craggy edges is exultation itself.

As the tides swell in their own colours, you are the cultural tourist watching their routes and rituals. It is merry sightseeing: their pubs, chippies, lotto merchants, programme sellers and catering vans. So very similar to what you know, and yet a different galaxy because they belong to these fans and this club. Their shop has the same items, and yet the colours and markings upon them mean they are from a parallel universe. From a distance their hero statues are similar, up close they are different species who scored goals on another timeline. *Vive la difference*, though: the very greatest thrill of the visit thus far is taking in the unique bends and folds of the ground's stands, its architectural nuances. Corrugated fibreglass or tin walls, red bricks and breeze blocks, odd doors with 'Press' or 'Directors' painted above them. Run your eyes upwards to windows and steel beams. Grounds often wear their innards on their edges, their ribcages displaying their history.

Because this is a day out, 'I Spy' can be deployed: five points for a steward needlessly searching an old lady's bag; ten for a turnstile operated by a human being . . . make your own rules, you're on holiday. Take in the concourse refreshment culture – three years after visiting, my mind remains blown that they sell brandy at Portman Road – and walk up the steps and into the light. That green. That flat meadow in front of you, a magic carpet, otherworldly. If this feeling ever dies, it is time to stop going to football.

When you've found your place, the ground's topography can be inhaled: the angles, gradients and fabric of seating; the press box and the noisiest area, the away cubby hole and the tunnel. The different roof heights and ages, the type of goal nets and dug-outs. This place is unrecognisable from the television version, fuzzy morning eyes finding their milk-bottle lens glasses. It is fresh and wonderful, a brief encounter for the price of train and match tickets.

Out march the teams, and the ground awakens, resuscitated. The sound it makes has a pitch and cadence of its own, part-affected by local accent and character traits. As the game lives out its life, your mind will drift, the upshot of hanging no hopes on either team. There is so much to occupy you, so many more swings and slides in the park. Watch the bawlers and the offended, the captivated and the bored children. Glance between the cracks and see the outside world – hills at Huddersfield or mosques at Luton.

When five o'clock comes, join someone else's trudge towards the train or the pub, and allow yourself to smile at this: after decades of giving your heart to football, it can still charm you daft.

24

PHYSIOTHERAPIST 'RACES'

Each match is a quilted mosaic of tiny pleasures. They are trifling and sporadic, and nothing compared with the ecstasy of a win, but they add a layer of gladness. Such pleasures can be found on the way to the game (patting a police horse) or inside the ground (cheering scores from elsewhere). They sparkle before the match (a warm-up shot hitting a fat club official in a suit) or during (the ball rebounding from the corner flag). My favourite – which seems to embody the way that something happening at a match makes it entertaining where elsewhere it wouldn't be – is physiotherapists racing one another.

Picture the scene: two players tear into a 50–50 tackle. Physics and misjudgement collide to leave both writhing around on the turf. Teammates rush around the referee, screeching blue murder. Managers and coaches pinball forward too, perhaps indulging in an 'unedifying' bout of finger-waving confrontation. Fans are similarly outraged, crying for sanctions. The physios see none of this. Perfectly still, boulders among ocean waves, they stare. All they see are players on the ground; wounded soldiers missing in action. At the signal of the referee, often before, they spring onto the pitch, eyes fixed on their two prone men.

They do not set out to race one another. The crowd has by now given up braying and noticed them. It is supporter cheers and jeers which define that this is a race. The physios are no more willing competitors than are greyhounds at the track. The noise rises, climbing further if the unfamiliar away team competitor has stumpy legs pumping like demented pistons. The fact he is carrying a bag containing undisclosed medical items enhances the charade. Onwards the two shunt, the lankiest creeping ahead. They both arrive at their players and this fleeting, daft moment is gone.

Shortly afterwards, one physiotherapist may make the international gesture for the bearing of a stretcher. The other will jog for the nearest touchline, help his player obtain the referee's attention, and dispatch him back into battle. Chest and heart clanking like hammer and tongs, he will saunter back towards the bench, always looking at his player, the departing vet glancing from his Land Rover at a repaired sheep, blind to the glee he has unleashed for some of us in the stands.

25

LOCAL LADS 'COMING THROUGH'

When I was a teenager, I startled a geography teacher. This had nothing to do with arable farming, and everything to do with European cities. During a test, it turned out that I knew the capitals of Serbia and Albania, Finland and Croatia. This was something of a surprise for me too. Behind my back, the European Cup and editions of *World Soccer* had sewn this knowledge into my brain.

Sometimes, this subconscious knowledge took me further than the Continent. I knew that Bulawayo could be found in Zimbabwe because Peter Ndlovu was 'the Bulawayo Bullet', and that the south of Brazil had cold winters because, via the pages of

90 Minutes magazine, Juninho told me so. Football's internationalism had struck.

At its best, this internationalism batters barriers aside and introduces us fans to people from outside our comfort zone, often before society gets around to it. Growing up, my football team was far more multicultural than the village I lived in. World Cups come along and make the planet seem united. Football is something we have in common with the farmer near Eindhoven and the student in Bogotá. Signings from around the world make us suddenly interested in, or at least aware of, its various corners and cultures.

And yet I will always prefer the local lad coming through.

I am almost embarrassed by this parochialism, this preference for chips over sushi, though I suspect I am not alone in feeling it. Local lads coming through matter. When they succeed, it means we are watching players we can relate to: we grew up where they did and speak like they do. It is likely that they too love the club beyond badge-kissing. We connect with them in a way we can't with signings. Local lads are distinctly of our community and bound by our shared will. We identify with them.

It often begins with a buzz. Word gets around of a 16-year-old who is a decent sort. He can't stop scoring for the youths, has played – and scored – for the reserves. In the past, we'd chart his progress via the matchday programme, and now we do the same online. Without having ever seen the lad play, we are pinning hopes on his undeveloped shoulders and demanding a five-year contract.

We remain transfixed by the romantic, matchday programme language surrounding players like this: 'local boy done good', 'rose through the ranks' and 'homegrown talent'. While crew-cut centre-midfielders from a bus ride away are still making the first team, football remains easy to comprehend and love.

There is charm in the way that they are forgiven many things outsiders aren't, appeal in the blinkered double-standards of loyalty. Limited skill never tarnishes admiration. Put a foot in and a clumsy back pass is forgotten. Indiscretion on a night out is just a trapping of local fame and staying put. He's one of our own, after all.

Local heroes often sparkle then burn. Their hometown careers are short and they leave, wending their paths down the divisions, drifters. They become a happy memory one night in the pub, and a figure about town. He may now be an electrician or a delivery driver, but still he has presence. He is one of us, and yet so much more.

26

I don't know why I need to know, but I do. I need to know that the attendance at Stranraer versus Brechin was 387, and I need to know the scoring sequence of Barnet's 3–2 win over York City. This information hardly matters by Monday, but on Sunday it is vital and crisp. I am unsettled, edgy even, until I am able to hold my eyes a few inches from the newspaper and gaze intently at tidings from Roots Hall and Plainmoor.

The double-page results spread is a work of art and a triumph of the factual. Nothing in the whole newspaper looks as good or is as accurate. There is no agenda, and content unites broadsheet and tabloid. It seems to offer so much information and take the reader to so many places, for a mere quid or two. No matter the carrier, these pages are always presented with a soothing symmetry, like looking at motorways from a night-time aeroplane. This combination of people and place names and numbers big and small forms a poetic code.

There are some conditions for prime inhaling of the results pages. The more detailed the spread the better; I always feel bereft when Scottish newspapers leave out English Football League attendances, and vice versa, as if they have been redacted by some meddling civil servant. Solitude is the best state for the full experience. To be asked a question by spouse, child or friend as you work out how many points Huddersfield Town need for safety is an intrusion of the real world. It can take a while to lose yourself anew in the Evo-Stik Premier scorelines.

When first I turn to these saintly pages, I take an overall look, as if standing back from a large painting in an art gallery. I need the reassurance of knowing just how many details are coming my way, and that even the Welsh League is here. Then comes a first walk through the scores, attentive eyes scouting for soft-spot teams and disliked ones. A second reading brings scrutiny of who scored where, and noticing familiar names, your exes on an old school photo. Those score spreads which still grant unto us full team line-up lists amplify this pleasant eavesdropping: among surnames and parentheses can we ascertain that loaned-out players came on for the last ten minutes when already the game was lost. There may even be player ratings. Those applied to a game you attended are ripe for enthralling scorn – 'bloody reporter can't have been there!'

The presence of goal times matters, too. They help you discern comebacks and consolations, as well as third-minute only-goals-of-the-game. Such examples fire intuition – you know that the rest of the match dragged laboriously.

These pages are carpeted in glorious architecture (half-time scorelines in brackets, referee names …), but it is attendance numbers I cherish most: surprisingly high ones in the Conference, and three-figure crowds that begin with a '1' in Scotland; pleasingly rounded numbers at Halifax and almighty thousands at Arsenal. Each of these figures is made of people spending their afternoons as I did, in every pocket and crease of the country. We disagree on fundamental things, and yet we are a synchronised movement.

Once the scores are absorbed the league tables are consumed. There is disappointment if it is early in the season and they are saplings, but in winter they sprout. At that point, they become storytellers, their PWDLFAPts plots classics to us. These are tales of hope, triumph, possibility, despair and middling along.

Still the bounty continues, gold coins dropping from a magic sky. First, top scorers lists and teams of the week. Then, the cosy thought that this is a long-running series with no final volume; that next week, you will do it all anew.

27

SHIRTS ON A LINE

One or two of the shirts will have faded. The colours themselves are often combinations unseen in professional football: orange and sky blue, black and white halves. They are more like the shirt colours depicted in birthday cards grandmas buy.

Their numbers ripple in the wind: a 7 belonging to the tiny winger who sits now in double maths and plots formations on the back of his exercise book, a 5 for the overgrown centre-half who every opponent thinks is a ringer. One size fits all, 15 shirts from the catalogue wholesaler, an outfitter of dreams.

It can be a straight, traditional washing line, pegs nipping the tops still, or a whirligig, spinning in the afternoon breeze. Like freezing changing rooms, crossbars riddled with scraps of duct tape, and pitches on a gentle slope, washed shirts are part of an enchanting landscape. Living among it are those who play the game for bliss and escapism alone, its highest form.

It is not just dreamy teenagers – the shirts can belong to a pub side or village B squads of seventh divisions. It will always be someone's turn to take the kits home, transforming a dispiriting muddy pile into neatly folded uniforms, another example of the weekly renewal which underpins all football. The faded left-back shirt and the number 14 with the rip under the arm will be packed into a holdall, ready for another try.

28

DEFENSIVE WALLS AND DROP-BALLS

The free-kick is given and the goalkeeper demands a wall. Backwards players trudge, little and large, to line-up like ragtag 1970s schoolboys about to be scolded by a headmaster. One of them turns to arrange the wall's position with his keeper, shuffling them left and right as if they were bound together by rope around their ankles. An opposing attacker or two may join the wall's end, or even stand in front of it. Their role is to decoy and distract in a game never afraid to be dirty or underhand, and all the more intriguing for that – imagine an action film without villains.

The goalkeeper hollers more instructions, measuring his angles from the sanctity of a post. To jump or not to jump, he must decide for his wall. Many a free-kick now zooms beneath the feet of hopping players, a cannonball hurtling towards the net. Still more are subtly curled, the up-and-under approach. All of that is very well, but the real delight in a defensive wall is when, somehow, it 'does its job', as commentators are robotically obliged to say. I am never sure if this is because the goalkeeper has organised the wall properly, or the free-kick is rancid, but there is something pleasing about such a base idea being so effective. It is, after all, some people made to stand in a line to try to stop an object passing.

If a thud can be heard then all the better, and if a secondary block is made by a charging brick from the wall, you have yourself a thrill. When clutching desperately to a one-goal lead, such events can inflame noise in a supporting crowd. Blocks are war cries, chest-beating actions. For a player to get a body part other than his foot in the way of the ball is noble. All opposition fans can do is weakly claim 'handball'.

Oh that drop-balls remained so fiercely contested. Still, even if most now end in long passes to

DEFENSIVE WALLS AND DROP-BALLS

opposition keepers, or kicking the ball out because of dreary fair play, they are worth celebrating as a cousin of the defensive wall: both are related as they are essentially a shrug of football's shoulders which says, 'We haven't thought of anything better yet.'

It helps their cause that drop-balls are often occasioned by sideshow events. I've seen them awarded following encroachment by streakers, the matchball bursting under the weight of a 50–50 challenge, and when the referee isn't quite sure what else to do.

In a classic drop-ball, that referee will warn those about to joust to wait until their target has reached the floor. He will hold the ball in his palm as if he were Hamlet and it poor Yorick's skull, before swiping away his arm and exiting left. In a flash, two footballers regress half a millennium and become the combatants in a medieval shin-kicking contest. With their feet they scrap for the ball like moles scratching at earth, blind to everything else. I suppose it is as close to rugby union as non-followers like me get. One player wins, play rumbles on, usually quickly climaxing with a throw-in. We are returned to the twenty-first century, but we have had a glimpse at pig's bladder games of yore.

These cousins are taken for granted, quiet and obscure delights which have an unfussy, functional beauty. They are further proof that no matter how much science and theory is applied to football, its greatest appeal rests in its simplest, instinctive pleasures.

29

CLUB ECCENTRICS

It is a broad church, ours, with room for all types. The football club connects a young web designer with an old lady who cleans the community centre for extra cash. It has room for the dedicated home-and-away pilgrim and the casual fan, even if the former scowls at the latter. You may have moved from the town long ago, your accent sanded smooth, but still you and the man who was born and will die within sight of the floodlights are welcomed alike. Club eccentrics are another piece of the furniture.

The club eccentric will be recognised by most who go to games. Some will even know his name, though it won't be that by which his mother addresses him, rather a moniker he may not even know about. He is usually alone, but there is no cause to feel sad or sorry for him: he is infatuated with a football club, and no human friendship could come close. He – and there are shes too – will be wearing an item of official club clothing, usually three or four years old. A hat is likely, pin badges clamped to the sides, as is a plastic supermarket bag of mystery items. This could be a more enduring carrier: I have seen battered rucksacks and even goalkeepers' kit bags used. The latter was stuffed with autograph books, and club eccentrics are often familiar with squiggle and pen. Via this pursuit, even the players come to know him. I wonder what he does in the week, let alone the empty summer, and picture eyes poking out from underneath a rubble of VHS club highlights tapes from the 1990s.

There are other forms of club eccentrics, not all of them as likeable. There is the noisemaker, a leader of the pack ready to stoke up a chant no matter the ground or scoreline. It is hard to like him if he takes off his top or, the team 4–0 down, turns to his fellow away-enders and berates them for not singing enough. Some eccentrics are drawn from outside the fanbase – the jolly, plump steward or the lotto man in a cowboy hat who sings of his wares operatically, which can be almost endearing on an optimistic day, hellish on a hangover. The garrulous whistling kitman whose 70th birthday merits a dug-out team mobbing after a goal is scored.

All of them are part of the pageant.

30

LOSING

It mustn't happen often, and to cherish it you probably have to like the melancholy of rain on a tent and sorry seaside towns on a Sunday evening. Losing in the right circumstances and at the right time can be a strange kind of delight.

It will usually be an away game (solace is hard to locate in home defeats). The travel element helps – you catch your reflection in a train window, looking a little destroyed. For a minute this is enjoyable because it is filmic and dramatic, you are the lovelorn star leaving small-town 1950s Pennsylvania on a Greyhound bus; you are alive, feeling, being. Then it is enjoyable because of the preposterousness of it all, a reminder that investing such deep emotions in a sport makes you a little bit ridiculous. Everyone needs that. Losing helps ground us.

Defeat is therapeutic, it gives reason to your anger, ration to the terrible mood you are in for the rest of the weekend. You have something to blame and, importantly, something to blame that can be put right with a win in seven days' time. No counsellor works at such speed. It makes other reverses through the week easier to take – bad news at work upsets colleagues but is nothing to you in comparison with the injury-time winner those bastards plundered last Saturday. You have perspective: a lost spreadsheet containing six months' work is nothing in relation to travelling 237 miles for a 5–1 defeat.

Indeed, there is even strange warmth in such a pasting. With each conceded goal, you move through the stages of defeat: annoyance but hope of an equaliser (1–0); perplexity at why your lads are suddenly so poor (2–0); anger (3–0); bemusement (4–0); and even black humour (5–0). You are not roaring with laughter, of course, but you have the darkly odd satisfaction of a man resigned to his fate, and the very useful emotion that things can only improve. And then they score a sixth.

I became aware that losing isn't always a bad thing in 1992. Middlesbrough had been hammered (and aren't the adjectives of defeat gratifying) 4–1 by Oldham Athletic. My friend's dad, Mr Moorhouse, was an Oldham man on whose industrial Lancastrian accent you could balance small rocks. Every word started with a capital letter. Detecting trauma – perhaps, for once, I wouldn't eat all of my oven chips – Mr Moorhouse set about outlining the philosophy of loss. 'Danny, lad. Sometimes they need a right kick up the backside,' he postulated.

The greatest luxury of defeat remains exactly what Mr Moorhouse was angling at: just how good the next victory feels.

31

WATCHING IN BAD WEATHER

It was the Scottish Cup final of 1889. Hampden Park was dressed in snow. Third Lanark and Celtic trudged on, slush nuzzling at their ankles. The players threw snowballs at one another. When the whistle went the game fired into life. Thirds won 3–0. From behind oak desks men in suits ordered a replay.

They were the bull-headed great uncles of those today who, every few years, propose that Caledonia embraces summer football. They were wrong then and they are wrong now. Football in bad weather is a deep joy. To forget that would be to abduct Christmas football and thieve from us the life-affirming sensation of shuffling from a searingly cold ground and into a cosy pub. Numb feet are a validator of commitment to the cause, a face turned stiff by pellet rain equally so. Ours is a game of sacrifice followed by sharp relief, a pastime that begins in daylight and ends under floodlights.

Bad weather can be beautiful. A playing field shrouded in snow makes the game a surreal act, as if the pitch has been turned inside-out. There may even be an orange ball, and hillocks of snow shovelled around the sidelines for over-zealous full-backs to plunge into. It ratchets up the entertainment too – the *frisson* of rumours that the game will be abandoned, footballs stopping dead on sodden grass, the magic words 'wind-assisted free-kick'.

Wearing a t-shirt alone to a match feels nude. This is a game of layers and scarves. Football *glows* in winter.

32

MY DAUGHTER LISTENING AT THE WINDOW

Every now and again, my daughter stands waiting by the back window of our living room. She points to the window handle and asks, 'Please can I listen to football now?' She wants me to twist that handle and let in the sound of Hibernian FC. Statistically, given that this request pops into her brain and out of her mouth at any time on any day of the year, Hibs are unlikely to be playing. It is pleasing that she believes football to be constantly going on, ready for her when she needs it, like CBeebies. When the odds smile upon us, though, we have ourselves an afternoon treat.

The wind must firstly tumble its way over Arthur's Seat, but, when all the angles are right, a spectacle that is heard and not seen bursts towards us. As the Tannoy recedes, we hear the pre-kick-off roar. My daughter's eyes widen and she stares up at me for explanation, though my words are nothing compared to the wonder ransacking her heart and the bemusement blowing at her ears like a possessed sea shell.

We hear early chants and away-end ripostes. It is easy enough to know what is going on via our sound portal: goals (the louder the reaction the more meaningful the goal); bad tackles from away full-backs (cries of guttural, primal outrage); refereeing mistakes (cries of incredulous, conspiratorial disgust). I try to explain the full sound library to my daughter, but only goals ever capture her imagination. 'Daddy, they GOALED . . . I think they GOALED. How do you goal again?'

Night matches offer other bewitchments. Roof-tops glow, basking in the offshoots of floodlights, and somehow the sound is clearer. We look from the other window and see a neighbour tying his green and white scarf in a knot and scampering down the front-yard path, still munching his tea. The idea of doing some-thing other than bath-pyjamas-teeth-bed-story-sleep when darkness falls transfixes her. Football is *naughty*. 'Why do they play football at bedtime, Daddy?'

For a stretch of my own youth, I dreamed about living near a football ground or, to be more precise, I dreamed about living near Ayresome Park. I wanted to be part of the family, not just an occasional visitor to the house. I imagined that living near Ayresome would grant me such a status. The ground would be part of my life; I'd see it from my bedroom window, walk by it on my way to school, hang around outside the Main Stand gates, probably kicking a ball about with my mates, and end up almost inevitably being scouted and signed up. It is possible that my daughter will feel the same about Easter Road stadium. Equally she may turn out not to like football, but I am clinging to the hope that her window-pointing gives me. Each time I put on my red and white scarf and head for the front door, she looks at me with a thousand eyes and asks, 'Please will you take *me* to football one day, Daddy?'

I will do my very best not to push my daughter towards football, not to be the Vulgarian child catcher offering lollipops and ice cream. If she does like the game, I will plead that I did not *make* her climb onto my knee to watch *Match of the Day* when she couldn't sleep, that it was *her* hand which pulled *mine* towards the sidelines of games in the park. I just didn't refuse, that's all.

Presently, the mere thought of her liking football stirs me. I am electrified by the possibility that pointing at the window may bloom into something we do together, and that here might be another human for whom football is a second heartbeat. That possibility in itself is a delight.

33

SINGING

Watching the game was like staring vacantly at a pond. When I think back, I don't picture passing and moving or huffing and puffing; I picture 22 men standing completely still. There isn't even a ball. Gateshead versus Bristol Rovers, the Heed and the Gas. Nil-nil, obviously, for most of the game anyway. In an away end far from home, eyes were double-glazed.

One supporter started singing, and before he had finished the first word, five or six more had joined him. By the second line of the song, hundreds were in on the round, most now standing, arms aloft. 'Irene, goodnight, Irene/Irene goodnight,' they sang in surprisingly arresting melody. 'Goodnight, Irene/

Goodnight, Irene/I'll see you in my dreams.' A reprise followed, and by now it was impossible to spy a soul who hadn't joined in the chorus. On this habitually dull February afternoon they had sprinkled romance around an athletics stadium set in an industrial estate. It wasn't just the content of the song, or the whirring Bristol lilt, that conjured this rosy sheen, nor the unity and shared sense of purpose. It was the uncomplicated jubilation of strangers singing, of base affection expressed.

To watch and listen is moving, to enrol in the choir can be spine-tingling. There you are, caught in the game, when a chant rises up. Your heart tells your mouth to join in, and because you do it feels like the whole world is singing. It can be a rushed call to arms or an anthem, a 'Come on, City' or a 'Blue Moon'. Often, it may only be one section of one stand, and yet it can still breed a sense of invincibility. When a song is broadcast from three or four sides of the ground the noise seems to drop from the sky and carpet the pitch.

Songs can fail, especially without a powerful originator. It is part of the choreography, like the strange way most fans know exactly when to end a repetitive chant, or the unspoken rule that no one must make eye contact while singing. When it works, when you are part of that ragtag choir, there is nowhere you would rather be.

34

BRACKETS IN SCORELINES

Ross County 7 [SEVEN] v 0 Falkirk. The vidiprinter spits out the landslide. If the results are being devoured somewhere communal then there are nudges, jeers and winces. Even when watching alone the brackets fizzle – you know because you wish there was someone else present to share them with you. This arguably unnecessary, possibly barbaric and definitely magnificent phenomenon survives, gratifyingly, in the modern era.

Brackets in scorelines are a graphic representation of humiliation. They are exclamation marks, wresting attention away from an exultant team which has just played the game of its life, and on to the sobbing wreck in the corner. They make the number they host become an incredulous shout. They loudly and slowly enunciate like an impatient middle-aged woman telling her half-deaf father how the microwave works. The brackets are a flare at sea, fluorescent arrows pointing, a pack of wolves howling, an air raid siren wailing, a foghorn honking, a child saying 'guess what?!' a thousand times, a white suit at a funeral, and an unsubtle stage direction. They make innocent, browbeaten teams the reluctant centres of attention, shy audience members picked out by a spotlight. Their defeat has been so absolute, so final, that it needs spelling out. Brackets twist the knife and then unleash a rifle just to make sure. They are particular, too; six goals and they leave the victim be, seven and sword is yanked from scabbard.

We enjoy the horror, but we also try to put ourselves in the shoes of the bracketed supporters. Are they pig-sick distraught or giddy at the gallows? Throwing scarves in service station bins or sinking delirious pints somewhere warm? Convinced of relegation, liquidation and other deathly hallows, or starting to imagine a tight back-to-basics one-nil win next Saturday? Perhaps later, they can even be proud of their brackets and grow to embrace them as a catalyst for optimism: once you've been bracketed, things can only get better.

35

STANDING ON A TERRACE

Off the top of my head: Accrington Stanley, Albion Rovers, Alloa Athletic, Annan Athletic, Arbroath, Ayr United, Barnet, Berwick Rangers, Brechin City, Brentford, Bristol Rovers, Burton Albion, Cambridge United, Carlisle United, Cowdenbeath, Crawley Town, Dagenham and Redbridge, Elgin City, Exeter City, Fleetwood Town, Forfar Athletic, Greenock Morton, Hartlepool United, Montrose, Morecambe, Newport County, Peterborough United, Peterhead, Queen of the South, Rochdale, Scunthorpe United, Stenhousemuir, Stevenage Town, Stranraer, Wimbledon, Wycombe Wanderers, Yeovil Town and York City.

This is not a relic. This is not wistful. You can stand on a terrace on any weekend this and every season.

One or two are lost each year yet, even today, wander among football league fields and it is not difficult to find a place to stand. The non-leagues are better still. Visit them, especially if you are a young fan who has known only shiny plastic. They breathe life into the wearied and the disillusioned, and help the new visitor view football through a different filter.

To pick your own place, ascend or descend bowing concrete steps and lean on a bar awakens something. It is innate, a sense that this is the natural way to watch football. Sitting is for the cinema. The match isn't passive like a film. You are part of it, you affect things, and standing is an active demeanour. When the ball hits the net and limbs bob and weave, you are reminded that the real action is in the stands. The same can't be felt as you shuffle by the half-arsed perma-seated old boy in the Main Stand, brushing up against his tartan blanket.

Where to choose? Palmerston Park, stately home to Queen of the South? Or Cappielow, where Greenock Morton go to dream? Or, yes, here's the place, Brunton Park, Carlisle, which has the very finest thing a football ground can have: a terrace running alongside the pitch. An obscure family holiday beckons.

36

WHEN THE BALL GOES IN THE CROWD

It's coming your way, it's coming your way, it's coming your way! Oh, but it lands just short, a few rows down and five or six seats across. The supporter who catches it does so perfectly and casts it pitchwards with a meaty, assured throw. Those around him pat his back and cheer. You ponder that in any case the ball would probably have smashed into your face, and that you're not even sure you can throw it that far.

The ball sails into the stands with the unpredictability of a comet. Being behind the goal during the warm-up increases your chances of receiving it but, in tandem, your chances of being concussed by it. When a wayward shot jolts into the stand during the match, there is just time for a jeer before it is parried around and returned, or in the odd away end concealed beneath a jumper until killjoy stewards retrieve it, luminous trading standards officers seizing counterfeit.

The finest specimen of the ball going into the crowd, though, is when a clearance – often by a goalkeeper – floats into a stand by the touchline. It allows a juvenile, communal thrill to build. For a moment, you are all back playing pass the parcel and feel that your turn is coming. In this instance there is, too, more time for the shared hope of contact to ferment, more time for reactions to be considered. When it reaches the stand, the lesser pace of the ball can mean clean catches and, on rare, golden occasions, headers. Cue chants of, 'Sign him on, sign him on, sign him on.' There are caveats which are seductive distractions in themselves: when the ball rattles around empty seats, and a ball boy has to pogo the advertising hoarding to retrieve it, and when it leaves the stadium altogether. Making a leap of consciousness, the latter gives you time to reminisce of childhood hours wasted trying to retrieve footballs from impenetrable gardens, spiky conifers and low-hanging Volvo estate cars.

This phenomenon pokes a hole in football's fourth wall. For a brief moment, the barrier between being part of the game and watching it tumbles. A full-back has to make eye contact with the child in the second row trying to return the ball, because he needs to take a throw and push his team towards an equaliser. Suddenly, the fan is a figment of the action and will remember those 15 seconds until grey and wistful.

37

KNOWING WHERE YOU WERE

I don't know why it matters. Life events should be significant enough in isolation without football fixtures clamping onto them like limpets.

On the afternoon I proposed to my wife, Middlesbrough were playing Manchester United in the FA Cup. We both have tender memories of sitting on a bench in Whitby that day, eating cheese and onion pasties. I also remember looking over her shoulder as we hugged, double-checking on a chalkboard that the game was going to be screened in the pub behind us.

My first kiss happened as Boro were beating Charlton Athletic 1–0. I was on a bus at the time. My parents split up the weekend we defeated

Blackburn Rovers, the reigning champions, and I lost my virginity the night before a derby win against Sunderland. I am glad that I became a father in the summertime, because I would hate to associate my daughter with an insulting home defeat.

Remembering these benchmarks with a match attached to them makes me feel retrospectively reassured about younger versions of myself. I know, through being inextricably linked to this football club, I had a certainty to see me through times of chaos and flux. Some people choose a star to look at in the sky. It makes them feel sure, fixed. We have dusty football grounds, mesmeric wingers and away wins that are etched within us like ancient cave paintings.

There is a more particular fulfilment in being able to say exactly where you were on a particular Saturday in 1993. Past fixture lists are an alibi, and you can precisely state where nine- or 16-year-old you was, and fairly accurately detect the mood you were in. Screw your eyes closed, drift away and you might just smell the Bovril.

It is all enormously comforting.

38

FOOTBALLESE

Every now and again, you see it. The picture in the newspaper or match programme shows a player who has just scored. He is in the penalty area, opponents spattered across the ground like dead flies, the goalkeeper's face unseen as he looks behind himself to survey the damage, a general grieving at the lookout post. This doesn't have to be a recent photo – it can be found decorating a flashback piece that warms your chest like tomato soup.

The scorer is spinning towards the halfway line, one or both arms climbing in self-salute. His eyes sparkle, his mouth is a boxing ring where a smile fights a hurrah. Your attention drifts downwards, to the caption beneath the image, the name upon the love heart, and you read how Tony Cottee or Don Goodman or Thierry Henry 'wheels away in delight'.

What a phrase. Like all the best Footballese, I have never seen it in any other context. Similarly, no politician, businessman or priest has ever 'issued a come-and-get-me plea' to a rival party, firm or religion. Wild sheep are never 'at sixes and sevens' like a chaotic defence, the parents of twins sadly don't 'bag a brace'. This is a language as useful and beautiful as Esperanto or some Greek mountain-whistling dialect, a rare gem.

Footballese is not the simple cliché; it is a lexicon, often written, and a glossary of adjectives (goal-getter, frontman, stopper, want-away midfielder). Whilst the cliché rises, Footballese appears to be in decline. The great hope is Scotland: here, its sister tongue has birthed words that have drifted into non-football use, a breeding programme for survival. Where once the 'stramash' was restricted to a goalmouth, now there is a political version. There can be a 'stooshie' outside the box too, perhaps even in the street. ('What's a "stooshie"?' I asked when

I moved to Edinburgh. 'Well, it's like a stramash, really,' someone replied.)

There is a subtle spoken dialect that derives from classic Footballese, kept alive by supporters. The way our team is 'we' and 'us' is quite particular: used by a fan it sounds warm; when someone describes their company in such terms it sounds like they have sold out or been indoctrinated. We know that what we sing is figurative – our lot aren't quite 'the finest team in football/the world has ever seen', it is just this golden vocabulary.

The next time you spy a fine example of our idiom, cut it out, pin it up, remind yourself: this game is poetry.

39

TIME-WASTING

Perching on the cliff of a 1–0 or a 3–2, this is how to stay alive. A free-kick in your own half offers the chance. 'Get it in the corner!' rasp voices in the crowd. Some, usually younger supporters, would rather garnish the afternoon with another goal. They are kamikaze pilots. The raspers know what is best, they know that the ball must be shepherded, not fired.

The free-kick is slung forward. Down by the corner flag, there are Buckaroo shenanigans. A raging bull of a full-back hacks and grabs at a centre-forward who has suddenly become an ox. He grows the shoulders of Quasimodo and is like a selfish ogre over the ball. His winger hurtles forward, a back-up plan. Quasimodo releases the ball, the winger rolls his foot over it a few times, toe-pokes it off the shin of the full-back, and it pings outwards for a corner.

Now must the corner-taker slowly jog over, digressing rather than progressing across the pitch. Quasimodo stays cornered. He and the taker urge 'yards!' from a defender or two. The ball is tip-tapped from taker to ox. Opponents bolt in, doubling and trebling up. They resemble a villain's henchmen, there to be batted aside with one kapow from Batman. Cue more Buckaroo limbs, more hacks and grabs and rebounds, throw-ins this time won. On and on, bleeding the game dry until the whistle.

I revel in the whole ritual, when on the right side, of course. It becomes more like a baying wrestling match, urgent and primal. That isn't to dismiss one of the happiest qualities of this – it takes skill. There is finesse in shielding a ball so conclusively, knowing exactly when to flick it onto a shin, and with trigonometric prowess enough to win a corner. It can be relished as an inverted ballet, athletic but simple to comprehend, and with bodies hunched as if ferociously hiding secrets.

Other time-wasting antics are awash with devilment, little boys pouring kettle water on ants. They are part of the pantomime and also bring pleasure. A goalkeeper waiting an age to launch his kick. As the referee hurries him on, he turns around his palms and curves incredulous shoulders, a wronged Parisian taxi driver. The referee gives him a long-distance booking from the edge of the box. A substitute leaving the pitch as if walking to the electric chair, and, of course, a felled player writhing on the ground, 'play-acting'. The referee is no bit-part: he ratchets affairs by showing that time is being added, gawping at his watch like a mime artist.

Here is a central theme of the plot that will never be encouraged in coaching manuals or praised in match reports. It is part of the guerrilla game, that underground, underhand version of football which runs beneath official narratives and belongs to the supporters. What a feeling when that 96th minute whistle peeps, and it peeps for you.

40

BEING AT A JUNCTION STATION ON MATCHDAY

You can loiter at Manchester Piccadilly, potter at Preston, idle at York or dawdle at Waterloo. A number of stations are good for this. Sit on a bench or outside the bar, and observe the rainbow of pilgrim supporters.

They gather beneath the departure screens, looking up at these unhelpful scoreboards. Some have plastic bags hosting lager and newspapers; those who have travelled further rest a rucksack on one shoulder, their hand on the strap. Many display a plumage of red and white stripes or deep blue, colours representing lives and hopes, and how far the wanderer has travelled, and that with some distance left to run.

They are crossing paths on behalf of their clubs, paths rarely shared – Conference fans and Premier

League. Sometimes these roaming ambassadors converse: 'Your lot are doing well, mate,' and, 'Who've you got today?' Sometimes they sneer. They are there for the same reason, just a different cause. Clock hands turn and they disperse, off to their corners for the day, marionettes guided by fixture lists. All chase the away win, which is sweeter when you've had to change trains.

Hours collapse, stations become less busy, speckled with closing flower stands and lonesomes waiting on dates. Diesel engines finally get a word in having been drowned out by bustle all day long, and information announcements are ringingly audible, as if the batteries in a communal hearing aid have been replaced. Then, from train doors and side doors, our breed emerges into the night-time railway station's peachy light. Groggy and disconsolate, delirious and beatific, the marionettes return with swift pints to be had, connections to make and the odd platform song to perform.

Once more they are gone, and next week different stripes will be worn. It is a warming kind of study, to watch ourselves like this, happy in our rituals and interactions, a social bunch.

41

COLLECTORS

In sheds, lofts and box rooms, museums are made. Open a cupboard door in one of these places, and you will find cardboard boxes, warping so that they rest at an italicised angle. Inside are items loosely connected to one football club. They have been stashed in there, loved of course, but piled up unthinkingly, a child's toy box rather than a time capsule. There will be programme bundles, scraps of paper with autographs on them, club mugs, pennants and retractable biros, portrait photos of players, old match tickets and concertina-folded fixture lists.

This is the haphazard, hoarding end of the scale, of items unthinkingly accrued over many years, the ramshackle volunteer-run town museum. Elsewhere on the scale is another type of collector altogether.

This collector has aims and an occasionally disturbing devotion to the cause. There is no dabbling, no scattergun approach. He or she will usually specialise in one or two areas – say, programmes and/or pin badges – and be stirred by the words 'unopened' and 'signed'. The collection will already be vast and orderly, neatly numbered – perhaps even partnered with a corresponding spreadsheet or ledger – and curated. There will be gaps, and while these remain the search will continue. The collector is alone on a dark and narrow lane, flashing a forlorn and hopeful torch into the hedgerows. Until he sees a Swindon Town away programme from 1932 or a ticket stub for a prestige friendly with Slavia Prague in 1965, he can never rest. Only when the final book is returned to the library stacks can he breathe easily, and then bolt the door behind him.

I celebrate this obsession. There are probably psychological reasons for it, but it is to be commended. While grasping for social acceptance stopped us collecting Panini stickers beyond our mid-teens, the collector retains the spirit we all once had. If an adult can preserve childlike wonder like this then it makes them privileged. There is, perhaps surprisingly for the stereotype of the collector, something punk about their pursuits – it is 'do it yourself' history, not owned by the club or those who claim to run the game. In piling up third kits or signed team posters, they are making sure we retain ownership of one element of our game at least: that which went before.

Whether a collector's archive is accidental or studied, all are united by the transportation that occurs when one clutches a brittle old programme or dusty international cap. Holding history in their hands takes them to another time, reinforcing their bond with this game in the present, as if recognising a likeness of themselves in the sepia photograph of a great-great grandfather. Collectors are not merely storing up ephemera for a rainy day. They are cultivating continuity and belonging.

42

FOOTBALL TOWNS

There is an easy and modern way to identify a football town: type the name of the place into a search engine, and see what tops the pile. If it is a webpage about the team, then this is usually a football town. Burnley, Bolton and Walsall . . . Watford, Derby and Barnsley . . . Middlesbrough, Rotherham and Ipswich . . . all are football towns.

This isn't to diminish other clubs, and especially not those from multi-team cities. After all, web algorithms have no feel for roars and trophies. Nor is it to suggest that football town teams matter more than any others. It is just that they often matter more in the life and perceptions of their surrounding area. Further, that area is small enough and the team's purchase on it strong enough to make matchdays in football towns a delightful experience.

When most football fans think of a place, they think of the team. With a football town, even those with only a faint interest in the game think, too, of the team. This can be due to past events or culture (milk and Accrington Stanley), but is often the result of osmosis via football results, caught or read accidentally. In many cases, the only time these places are mentioned nationally is in the reading of results. They are often post-industrial towns where the football club has become a beacon and something to cling on to. As people can no longer anchor themselves to a factory or shipyard, they cling to their football club. Identities become joined, and the team and town are one. For better or worse (what happens if the club disappears?), that is impossible in most large urban areas.

In the clockwork of the football town itself, the club is not just about those who shove the turnstile. It is part of the fabric. Your hairdresser and your grandma look out for the results, and were probably at the bigger games as children. The names of local taxi firms and chip shops reference the team, and it is the centre-half, not the mayor, who cuts the ribbon and declares supermarkets open.

On matchday, a football town is vivid. The air is different, the streets busier, clarets or stripes swarming. It makes many a flagging economy appear healthy. Every watch seems to be set to the same time of three o'clock, whether its wearer is going to the game or not. It is the hour when the pubs will quieten and the town will go back to sleep. Until then, it seems like everything and everyone is heading towards the ground.

A football town blooms best during a rare run to a Cup or play-off final. In the newsagents there are window displays, the butcher has made a special Wanderers pie, the bakery a cake declaring its best wishes in icing. Bring home the prize, and at the open-top bus parade the team and town will melt into one.

43

STRIKING UP A FOOTBALL CONVERSATION ON A SOCIAL OCCASION

If friends or relatives are unworldly enough to get married before the end of May, your fellow travellers are easy to detect. As three o'clock comes and goes, they will be mauling their pockets for mobile phones, taking shifty looks at them during the endless parade of wedding photographs then full-on glances as the father of the bride makes his speech. Later, when images of the wedding surface, they can be recognised, surly in the background. It may appear as if they are jealous, that they should be marrying bride or groom. Actually, they have just received a text which says, 'Lost 2–1, love, Dad.' The score must be known, no matter who is offended.

Things are more difficult in June and July – unless you can strike lucky while sidling along the evening buffet and verbalising an unlikely link between Sheffield United and couscous, everything is clandestine, everyone undercover. The surest way in is by asking a stranger where they are from, and moving things quickly to the local football club. The code words for bringing this speed date to an abrupt end are: 'Yeah, I'm not really into football.' When a match is made romance is sudden, the words 'season ticket for 27 years' dirty talk. You are in.

Whatever the month, the moment of connection is delicious. There you are, one minute strangers, the next discussing a former right-back's cruciate ligament. It works everywhere, a profound demonstration of football's universality. You can have nothing in common and suddenly everything. The cake is being cut but you have away-day memories to trudge through, the first dance is barely seen as one of you remembers a bald centre-midfielder that played for both of your clubs. It makes the many long pauses of a wedding day drift away unnoticed. Midnight comes and you go your own ways, ending a romance within a romance.

44

SOLID FIXTURES

I don't wish to attend the games or watch them on television, I am just happy to know that they are there. Spurs versus Everton, Newcastle United versus Aston Villa, Stoke City versus West Bromwich Albion, Nottingham Forest versus Wolves. Solid, unflinching fixtures, homely like Sunday dinner and sitting in your dad's shed. The teams that contest them are plucked from a Subbuteo world where time stands still. Reading their names set together is like perusing a menu featuring only school-dinner desserts. They are custard teams.

There is little evolution, and no new club can ascend to the realms of the solid. Team colours rarely change, just shirts, sponsors and hairstyles.

Solid fixtures are a constant, the games they serve up seldom shocking or thrilling, but always sure. They will be watched by similarly solid crowds: numbers never beneath 20,000, noise if not deafening then distracting.

Certain lower-league fixtures embody this in their own way, though they are difficult to list. This is not least because the nether divisions are more mobile, truer meritocracies. You only know they are solid when you read or hear of them: Rochdale versus Scunthorpe United, Gillingham versus Colchester United. Those names together engender a distanced warmth, like hearing an old acquaintance is doing well. 'Tell Oldham and Port Vale I was asking after them . . .'

Solid fixtures reinforce the feeling that football has always been there, and always will be.

45

CLUB NICKNAMES

The Shrimpers and the Brewers . . . the Blades and the Chairboys . . . the Potters and the Glovers . . . football nicknames that speak of local industries are entrancing and intriguing. They are made from cosy words that would ease comfortably into music-hall lyrics. They remind us that clubs walk hand-in-hand with their surroundings, and recall trades and factories dead and buried, like newborn babies with the middle name of a great-great grandad. In Northampton can we see Cobbler ghosts tapping and tacking shoes? In Walsall, Saddlers dressing horses? Nicknames are geographic encyclopaedias, too – only through them did I learn that Reading was once famous for making biscuits, Kidderminster for carpets, that Chesterfield's church had a crooked spire and that there were lots of Quakers in Darlington.

Then there are animal nicknames that take us into a British summertime fairytale kingdom of Bantams and Bees, Magpies, Hornets and Owls. Many of these derive from kit colours, as if a child had pointed at a red shirt and blurted out, 'Robin!' It all adds to the wonderland feel of nicknames, that they are football in a parallel universe, kinder and wholesome. The Yellows of Mansfield and Oxford, the Blues of Birmingham and Ipswich, and the Hoops of Shepherd's Bush are all at the tea party too.

Scotland's stars hang in different clusters. They are often stroked by romance – Ayr United's Honest Men fell off the page of a Burns poem; Queen of the South are the Doonhamers, named from exiles in Edinburgh and Glasgow longing to scarper 'doon hame' to Dumfries. Most refer to aspects of their town rather than what it made: Red Lichties of Arbroath after a lighthouse, Hedgemen of Brechin after fine topiary and Bairns of Falkirk after the town's creaking Latin motto. The handle that sings most to me is Clyde's. There is no clear truth as to why they are nicknamed the Bully Wee, and I like that you can make of it what you wish. I think of a tenacious cartoon character, biting the ankles of his enemies, all the time wearing Clyde's white shirts and black shorts.

All are merely words, and many of them rarely used, but nicknames add texture to football, and sometimes give it a much-needed, rosy glow.

46

THE 'HECTIC CHRISTMAS SCHEDULE'

There we sit like Roman officials at the Colosseum, sated and bloated. It is Boxing Day in a football ground, and all we can do is sprawl over the plastic, hurling instructions and vague encouragement. The seat is an extension of the sofa, the match another Pick of the Day in the *Radio Times*. Some are wearing Santa hats, some have been drinking only six or seven hours after last stopping, guzzling away, topping up their levels to reach pie-eyed delirium. The scents are best left unwritten.

For once, jealousy is suspended and we have something over the players. While they were at the training ground or on a coach yesterday, we were free to listen to our families bicker. Matches, the programme notes remind us, come 'thick and fast' at this merry time of the season, and some players skirt as close to meriting their wages as they ever will. On the 23rd and the 26th, the 29th and the 2nd, footballers are among the most productive workers in Britain.

'Good Christmas?' we ask one another. If we're honest we admit we spent much of it being relieved that there was a match to escape to the next day. Nothing gets an overly inquisitive auntie or an uncle with unpalatable political views off your back like a Boxing Day fixture. Football is always an escape, but it is a literal one at Yuletide. If you can't get to the game, there is always a radio to jam your ear against in a forgotten corner of the living room. Even *Soccer Saturday* with the mute button pressed feels like jumping into a high-speed getaway car.

Down in the concourses at half-time, football and Christmas collide to make excitable children of us all. There is probably a bigger crowd than usual. It is swelled by home-comers from London, Aberdeen and abroad, bumping into old pals and old flames, sipping with seldom-seen kid brothers. It becomes a grotto, hubbubbing with more noise than any class on a school visit could make, the air mobbed by breathless chatter about life and the transfer window.

For away-team supporters on Boxing Day, this dance is a pleasure delayed. A few days later, the party is in their house. Everything is repeated, except the railways have reopened, meaning grander away followings. On board, as the carriages meander among retreating snow, livers turn dismal and throats crimson, but still there is nowhere a supporter would rather be. Home fans get their turn at last, crawling from the front door and into the light, waking as if from hibernation, dancing by overflowing wheelie bins across icy pavements towards the ground, and the best of the holiday yet. Football just feels right at this time of the year, in the same way that emailing or eating salad doesn't.

Onwards she marches, battering you over the head with a match quickly after New Year's Eve. Who needs Alka-Seltzer when seven points out of nine are snaffled? All these games, after all, disguise a season moving onwards and upwards, progressing rapidly. This period is not all hangovers and style. There is substance to it, technical purpose. Then comes FA Cup Third-Round day, the very greatest song saved for the encore.

Such is football in the season of goodwill. It should not be changed any more than Christmas itself should.

47

OUTFIELD PLAYERS IN GOAL

The substitute goalkeeper leads a lonely life. He is only called upon when something goes wrong – a paramedic in a number 13 shirt – and exists as something of a legal obligation. Even when he is outsourced by way of a loan to a smaller club, it is to fill in for someone else and then return home, a row added to his appearances panel on Wikipedia. The loan club's manager will probably have saluted his 'professionalism', but still the bench beckons once more.

Then one afternoon his fellow goalkeeper is clattered while rising to pluck a corner from the air. He is told to warm up. He stretches and wishes concussion – just a mild one – upon his teammate.

The sign is given, off comes his tracksuit and on he sprints, stopping by the number one's stretcher to check there is definitely no pulse. I should be happy for him, the patient understudy finally giving us his Hamlet. And yet I resent him. I resent him because the very existence of the substitute goalkeeper has half-ruined one of football's perfect diversions.

There is nowadays very little call for an outfield player to go in goal. Instances are rare since some bureaucrat, blind to slapstick, created an emergency service by allowing far too many substitutes. However, there are just enough circumstances to make the scenario plausible, if unlikely, and so well worth crossing your fingers for: a sent-off goalkeeper followed by an injured one; no substitutions left to make; or no goalkeeper on the bench. All such cataclysms of misfortune can lead to this spectacle. Roll up, roll up for the cabaret.

If this unusual firework is lit, the atmosphere in the ground will be crackling. All the better if an injustice has caused the anomaly – from adversity comes volume. When the candidate emerges – 'He's always mucking about in goal at training,' you hear in post-match interviews – the first part of the performance can begin. For some reason, a goalkeeper's shirt is always too big for an outfield player. It flaps baggily in the wind, and laps towards the ends of his shorts. He pulls on gloves drenched heavy by sweat, yanking the Velcro wrist straps tight with his mouth, and only then begins to tuck in his shirt. It is like shoving a flag into a drain and when he is finished, he still resembles a schoolboy dressed from the lost-property box. Once he has jumped up to demonstrate – to himself as much as anyone else – that he can reach the crossbar, play can begin.

Often, an outfield player in goal's first act is to face a penalty. This means a prompt opportunity to witness his diving style. There will be plenty more as opponents sniff fear and blood. That style is usually exaggerated rather than controlled. He is a civilian throwing himself on an unexploded bomb. He seems to move like a child's lost helium balloon, zigzagging wildly according to the whims of a gust. Elbows and knees are engaged, jazz hands rigid. Some shots fly by him, many more hit various spots on his body and cannon against the bar or out for a corner. Nothing is of greater use to the outfield player in goal than the kick-save. 'Use your hands!' the crowd cry as they did at reluctant street keepers in childhood. He rarely will. It is a basic reflex for him, even if he looks as though he is being controlled by strings from above.

The whole episode makes for chaotic, unbridled fun. It reminds us that all footballers are descendants of 25-a-side contests in the park. The frolics of these have-a-go heroes rekindle in everyone, on and off the pitch, a childlike, raw love of the game.

48

SEEING A TEAM BUS

This is best on a motorway, and when the team you catch sight of isn't one you are on the way to see.

There is something reassuringly old-fashioned in the way clubs still travel by coach. It feels like a remnant from another era, albeit one with microwaves and televisions that squash Jeff Stelling's head into an oblong. Many players would probably rather rocket to games in one of their three cars, and I like that the club coach must make them into surly teenagers, resentful at having to travel with Mum and Dad, peashooting the back of the reserve team manager's head through a McDonald's straw.

Some have branded buses, but most seem content with a Perspex rectangle slammed up against the windscreen that reads 'OFFICIAL COACH OF BIRMINGHAM CITY FC' or 'BRENTFORD FOOTBALL CLUB TEAM COACH'. As they slide into view it somehow quickens the heart, but then that could just be a symptom of how bored I get on motorways. You can catch a glimpse of centre-midfielders and goalkeeping coaches in real life, which is always something. They are bored, just like you, only slightly higher up.

What do they talk about, I wonder? Football? House prices? Slightly odd men in the passenger seats of cars staring at them? Then they are gone, their card schools in full flight, some players talking, some not, the kitman napping with his head against the window. It's almost like they are normal humans.

49

WATCHING PEOPLE GET PLAYER AUTOGRAPHS

The football ground is being tucked in and put to bed for another week or more. Where an hour ago hails and groans spiked the afternoon, evening quiet cloaks all, save for the noises of the wind-down. There are odd clanks and bangs as things are sorted and locked, nursery toys being tidied away now that the children have left for the day. Inside, the groundsman is tutting and stabbing, the nets are tied to the crossbar while seagulls eye up piles of litter. Reporters file, referees deodorise, managers comb thinning mops and players make social plans.

Among the autograph-hunters outside, stewards and catering staff say goodnight, unidentified older gents in club ties scurry from the main reception, and tracksuited youth team players away home or to Nando's. It is a neglected, fascinating time to be around a football ground, but the autograph-hunters don't notice. They are primed, leaning on steel barriers, eyes on a door marked 'Players and Officials'.

In notches the sky darkens. The match ended in British dusk: not yellow, hazy and warm as on holiday, but blue, crisp and cool. In winter it climbs from the pleasing shade of Yorkie bar wrappers, to the daunting navy of a security guard's uniform. There is a particular kind of cold outside a football ground at Saturday tea time. The air can be perfectly still but it manages to wrap itself around you, toe to nose. It infiltrates your body, sneaking through sleeves and ear canals to freeze extremities and brains, and it neutralises catering-van scents. Still the hunters don't notice.

There they are, two distinct tribes: the older gentleman in his sensible coat and bobble hat, and the gaggle of children and young teens, some with mums or dads a few feet behind. The seniors move alone and are organised, autograph books and team posters clipped to card or cork. In flocks the youngsters waggle a programme or a mobile phone, a selfie with a player more the prize than a scribble. Should they miss a sneaky hero, there is always the chase across the car park, and among the warren alleys between the shiny Beamers and the tinted Jeeps, and the yelling of a player's name.

The door creaks open and the race is on. Most players sign, a washbag tucked beneath an arm, headphones around the neck. They are helping collectors accrue and young fans go starry-eyed. Pen on paper or finger on button, five seconds that make worlds go round.

50

THE LAST DAY OF THE SEASON

To the ground, one last time. The end is nigh. All that football we blinked through, those bank statements we hid, and the dirty old towns we found ourselves in, itinerant salespeople dispatched to every nook and cranny of the land in search of gold. August hopes usually seem remote, though if we've wished upon a star and he's given us 27 goals, on this end of days utopia may be in sight. And where there is 'mathematical possibility' there is hope.

Thus is the last day divided between the many playing for nothing, and the few groping for everything. For the fruitless and the hopeful, final days happen at two speeds in different dimensions. They are of the same sport and earth, but not of the same time or movement. The crowds say it all: in one place beachballs are pawed around; in another promotion- or relegation-anxiety robs years from people.

When the last day matters we feel like we are the earth's core. When it doesn't, we are a decaying satellite. Still, we can revel, revel as the nightwatchman of a club on the cusp of change. Players, or whole board regimes, may depart in the summer, and today is ripe to survey the wreckage and peer towards the horizon from the crow's nest behind the goal. Then there are scores from elsewhere bearing the pain of others, wartime telegrams delivered to the wrong door. It is fleshy, wonderful and voyeuristic, like tonight's *Match of the Day*, where vital games are shown not in sequence, but interspersed with one another to make a melodrama, on-screen league tables fluctuating with the peppering of goals.

These, though, are withdrawn pleasures, and deep down we all crave the headrushes and bonecrushes of the supporter surviving a game that matters. Lose it and he'll never feel more like death; win it, and he'll never be more alive. He'll pogo and jive, hurdle barriers and evade stewards, feign headers in the penalty area as a pitch invasion unfurls.

In the days that follow, both groups, both dimensions, become united. Time tapers and slows for all of us. The first couple of Saturdays feel like a holiday, the next few a vacuum. Summer is a burden, two empty months.

The sun sets, but we all know morning will come again soon enough, bold as brass and brighter than ever. The birds will chirp to a new tune. That's football's genius. It never really ends.

ACKNOWLEDGEMENTS

For their love, patience and bringing in bowls of wine gums without interruption while I was writing, Marisa and Kaitlyn; for wisdom and persistent support, Mark Stanton of Jenny Brown Associates; for faith in my words and always improving them, Charlotte Atyeo at Bloomsbury; for support and seeing this one over the line, Holly Jarrald at Bloomsbury.

And a tip of the flat-cap to three great Yorkshire folk: Mum, Dad and JB Priestley.